Breakthrough Prayers For Our Parents

Written By
Julian Businge , Sheila Burum, Angella S. Batebe , Mary Roche

© Copyright 2021

All Rights Reserved.

The Purpose Of This Document Is To Provide Accurate And Reliable Information On The Topic And Issue At Hand. The Book Is Sold With The Understanding That The Publisher Is Not Obligated To Provide Accounting, Legally Permitted, Or Otherwise Qualified Services. If Legal Or Professional Advice Is Required, A Well-Versed Professional Should Be Consulted.

All Intellectual Property Rights Are Reserved.

All Copyrights Not Held By The Publisher Belong To The Authors.

ISBN: 978-1-8381372-6-7

Table Of Content

BOOK OVERVIEW 5
DEDICATION 8
ACKNOWLEDGEMENT 9
Chapter 1 10
  1.1 What Is A Breakthrough PRAYER? 10
  1.2 Importance Of Breakthrough Declaration 20
Chapter 2 25
  How Praying For Breakthrough For Parents Works 25
Chapter 3 28
  1.1 Prayer For Parent Health 28
  1.2 Praying For Those That Are Struggling 37
Chapter 4 45
  Pray Against Their Enemies 45
Chapter 5 51
  Pray God To Send Them Helpers 51
Chapter 6 58
  Pray For God's Protection For Them 58

Chapter 7	67
Pray For Their Investment	67
Chapter 8	74
Pray For Their Pension	74
Chapter 9	82
Pray For Parents Not To Lack	82
Chapter 10	92
What Does The Bible Say About	92
Chapter 11	106
Scriptures To Pray Over Your Family	106
Chapter 12	118
Godly Story About Parental Love	118
Conclusion	121

BOOK OVERVIEW

A big thank you to every parent who has been praying for their children. Our parents and guardians are known to spend their entire lifetime praying for their children, but we, as children, it's upon us now especially as adults too to pray for them, especially as they get weaker in their bodies. There Are Times In their lives When they, too, Need a breakthrough, no matter their age. Our parents may require a few answers for a Breakthrough In a Project Or Business adventure. When our parents Transition To The Next Stage Of Their Lives, It Can Be A Watershed Moment. There Are Times When they may feel trapped and have No Idea What To Do.

And What We Most Want for them Is a smile, joy after receiving a Miracle or a Breakthrough will be a game-Changer. Most Of The time, When our parents are at a Crossroads in their Lives, We as children may not Know What to Pray for during that difficult moment. Are You a parent In Desperate Need Of A Miracle Right Now? Do you

Need Some Prayer Points With Bible Verses To Pray?

There Are Numerous Ways To Pray. But, Among Prayers For Comfort, Peace, And Healing, One Form Of Prayer Is Frequently Mentioned: A Prayer For a "Breakthrough." What Exactly Is A Breakthrough, And How Should We Pray For One?

The Broad Concept Of A "Spiritual Breakthrough" Refers To Attaining A New Level Of Spirituality. In General, A "Breakthrough" Is A Quick, Dramatic, And Significant Discovery Or Development Or Achievement Of Success In A Certain Sector Or Activity. A Breakthrough Occurs When A Person Is Saved, Has A Greater Grasp Of Biblical Truth, Receives An Answer To Prayer, Or Triumphs Over Sin.

When God Speaks, Darkness And Death Tremble! His Voice Possesses The Most Potent Force In The Cosmos. And He Has entrusted his children With The responsibility Of Declaring What He Speaks And Saying What He Says. It Is Time For Believers in Christ Jesus to respond to the Enemy's

Attacks, Always in the form of Liars and accusations, With God's Words Of Truth To Bring Freedom To All Who hear.

DEDICATION

To our dear mother, Lucy Sabiiti, we appreciate you. To all our beloved parents and guardians worldwide. You are all unique treasures. It is the right time for all children to stand in the gap to lift our parents in prayer.

May our parents fully enjoy a blessed life at its best.

ACKNOWLEDGEMENT

God Bless you all who have made this publication possible and may God's Kingdom come through you. We thank the HolySpirit for inspirations and guiding us.

CHAPTER 1

1.1 WHAT IS A BREAKTHROUGH PRAYER?

Breakthrough prayer is in Christian Communities As A Period When A Person Is Saved, Develops A Greater Grasp Of Biblical Truth, and receives an answer to prayer or triumphs over a vexing Sin. For Example, Paul's encounter in the Bible on the

Damascus Road is a Breakthrough Because It Allowed Him To See Jesus For The First Time (Acts 9). On the rooftop Of Joppa, Peter's encounter is A breakthrough prayer, As He Discovered That The Gospel Was For Everyone, Including Gentiles (Acts 10). When Believers in Christ Jesus feel Disconnected From God, they may desire A Breakthrough prayer. Many Christians Believe That They Require A Consistent emotional Response During Worship Or Prayer and that If they do not get that experience, there is Something Wrong With Them Or God Has Left Them For Some Reason. However, it Is Incorrect Thinking. According To The Bible, God Is love, we are one in his love (Romans 8:37–39), And We Can Rest Happily In His Promise, "Never Will I Leave You; Never Will I Abandon You" (Hebrews 13:5). We as children may be far from our parents, but love still holds us together as one.

It Is The Same In Our Connection With God. Emotional And Spiritual Highs Do Occur. We Occasionally Receive Spectacular Answers To Prayer, Moments Of Extraordinary Insight, Or Intense Delight. But They Are Only The Icing On The Cake—so delicious, But Not The essence Of our Connection. If We Focus On The Highs, We May Miss The Wonderful, Peaceful Periods In The Valley When God Works Unnoticed, And We May Not Have Great Insight. Rather Than Focusing On Our Own Experiences, We Should Pray With Patience And Perseverance for our parents That God Will Finish The Good Job He Began In Whatever Way He Deems Fit (Philippians 1:6).

Breakthrough Declarations

No weapon devised against our parents Shall Prosper, And Every Voice that rises in Judgment against our parents Shall Be Condemned." We destroy satan's works over our parents. This is The Inheritance Of The Lord's People, Says The Lord"

(Isaiah 54:17).

"The Lord Will Battle For our parents While we Keep our Peace," Says The Lord. 14:14 (Exodus 14:14)

"As A Result, our parents Devote themselves To God." "our parents are Resisting The Devil, And He Will Run From them." 4:7 (James)

"The Lord, He Goes Ahead Of them." He'll Be There With our parents. He Will Not Let our parents Down Or Abandon them. "We Shall Not Be Afraid Or Disheartened" (Deuteronomy 31:8).

"our parents Will Pray To The Lord, Who Is Worthy Of Honour, And our parents Will Be Delivered From their Adversaries" (Psalm 18:3).

"Even Though our parents Walk Through The Valley Of The Shadow Of Death, they Will Not Be Afraid; For You Are With them; Your Rod And Your Staff Comfort our parents."

Psalm 23:4

"Whom Shall our parents Fear If The Lord Is their Light And their Salvation?" "Whom Shall they Fear Because The Lord Is their Strength?" (See Psalm 27:1).

"The Lord's Angel Encamps Around Those Who Fear Him And Delivers them" (Psalm 34:7).

"In Times Of Trouble, our parents Call On God; HE Will Deliver them, And they Will Glorify Him" (Psalm 50:15).

"I Called To The Lord In our parents' Pain, And He Freed our parents from Their Affliction." He Rescued them From The Shadow Of Death And Severed Their Ties. We, Will, Give Thanks To The Lord For His Goodness And His Amazing Works Among The People! For He Has Shattered The Bronze Gates And Slashed The Iron Bars In Half" (Psalm 107:13-16).

"Through God, We Will Be Courageous, Since He Will Tread Down their Foes" (Psalm 108:13).

"But Praise God, Who Gives our parents Triumph Through Our Lord Jesus Christ!" (1 Corinthians 15:57.)

"Look, our parents Have Permission To Trample On Serpents And Scorpions, As Well As All Of Their Enemy's Might." And Nothing Shall In Any Way Harm them" (Luke 10:19).

Prayer Point

Father in heaven, we come together with our parents, we repent of all our sins and admit That we are all sinners and saved by Grace today. There are many times we have Intentionally And Inadvertently Sinned Against You. Please Have Mercy On us all And Forgive our Faults, Lord. In Jesus' Name.

Father, Do Not Let our Sins and those of our fathers Stand In The Way Of our Breakthrough prayer. Proverbs 28:13.

Lord, we Pray For our parents' Breakthrough In their Life; please Bring Your Will And Promises For their Life To Fruition In Jesus' Name. 1John5:14-15

In The Name Of Jesus, we Decree Manifestations of all Of God's Blessings And Favour In the Life of our parents. Ephesians 1:3-3.

Father, In The Name Of Jesus, we Come against every Arrow And trap that anyone Or The Adversary Has Laid To Damage our parents' Life Or Pervert their Plans And God's Blessings For our parents' Life. We Come Against Every Accusation Of The Devil, Every Decree, Voice, And Every Word Said Against our parents' Destiny, And we Triumph Over the works of satan through The Blood Of Jesus. Read Isaiah 54:17 And Revelations 12:11. Father, May Your Glory Shine On our parents' Life, Career, Marriage, Family, Academics, And Business. In The Name Of Jesus. Read Isaiah 60:1–2.

As we Come In Obedience To God And His Word, we Hope That All The Days Of Difficulty In our parents' Life Are Over And That they Will Spend their Days In Prosperity And their Years In Pleasure In Jesus Name. Job 36:11.

Lord, Go Ahead Of our parents And Make Every Twisted And Hazy Path In their Life Clear And Straight.

Allow our parents To Recognize the Many Opportunities In their environment, mutually beneficial partnerships, opportunities, charities And The Things they need to do To Experience unlimited Financial increase that they may leave an inheritance to their great-grandchildren And Live In Abundance. Isaiah 45:2-3, Proverbs 4:18

Lord, In the Name Of Jesus, Grant our parents The Grace To Live In Obedience To Your Word, To Live A Righteous Life That Your Blessings Will Materialize In their Life Without Impediment. Read Romans 12:1-14 And Deuteronomy 28:1-14.

Father, Bless our parents' Hands, Let All they Put their Hands To do Succeed, And Make The

Country our parents live in Fertile For them. In The Name Of Jesus.

Father, Allow our parents To Eat And Enjoy The Bounty Of The Land they live in. Deuteronomy 28:12, Isaiah 1:19.

Lord, make way for all our parents and guardians Where There Appears To Be No Way, A Hope Where There Appears To Be No Hope, Possibilities Where Everything Appears To Be Impossible, In Jesus' Name. Isaiah 43:19.

1.2 IMPORTANCE OF BREAKTHROUGH DECLARATION

The Term "Breakthrough" As Used in this book Is Personal And Quite Specific To Each Individual, family, parents. For Some, A Breakthrough Might Mean Salvation. Others May See It As Debt-Freedom. To Another, It Could Mean Breaking Free From The Bonds Of Fear. The Number Of Alternatives Is Endless. But With The Lord's Power, What Binds You Or Your Loved One Will Not Last Forever.

The Truth Of God's Word Is The Most Powerful Tool For Breaking Free From Bonds. According To John 8:32, It Is The Truth Of The Scripture - God's Exact Words – That Makes Us Free. When We Hold To The Hope Of God's Promises, Chains Fall Away. A Breakthrough prayer Occurs When We Seek God's Will ,intervention And Put Our Trust In Him. Furthermore, Prayer Is A Potent Weapon Against That Which Holds Us Captive. When We Pray The Truth Of Scripture, We Are Claiming God's Promises And Returning Them To Him. "A Righteous Man's Prayer Has Immense Power To Prevail." James 5:16 . Because Of The Power Of The Ruach, The Prayers We Pray Result In Significant Breakthroughs In Our Lives and that of our parents and guardians.

Things That enslave Us Have No Place In Our Lives nor our parents. We Must Give Up Everything That Has A Place In Our Hearts That God Should Have. Whether It's The Salvation Of A Family Member, Debt That's Tying our parents Down, Fear That's Keeping them From Sharing The Wonderful Hope In Yeshua, Or Anything Else, Those Strongholds Must Be Surrendered To

The Lord In Truth And Prayer. And With The Power Of The Ruach, we Will See Powerful Breakthroughs In our parents Life ,guardians And The Lives Of People Around them.

Your Declarations

As we pray for our parents, we Declare That God Has Spoken Through us. Our Words are Spirit And Life Because Christ Is In us. When we Speak, we Have The Power To Transform our World and that of our parents.

Our Remarks Are Strong And Filled With The Holy Spirit. Miracles Happen When we pray. Our Mind Is On What Is Pure, Lovely, Just, And Noble. We Shall Talk In A Way That Is Life-Giving Rather Than Death-Dealing.

We Shall Strengthen our Faith In The Lord And Carry Out His Will For our Lives and parents. We are all Powerful through Christ Jesus. We are Capable, because He Loves us all so much, we are More Than Conquerors in Christ. We Declare God's Peace Over our parents Life And guardians: Nothing Is Missing, Broken, Or Harmed. Our parents Will Chase, Overtake, and Reclaim Whatever The Adversary Has Stolen From them. In "Open Your Mouth With A Tremendous Decree; our parents Will Accomplish It Today,

You Will See!" So Shall It Be With The Words You Speak. Psalm 81:10 .

CHAPTER 2

HOW PRAYING FOR BREAKTHROUGH FOR PARENTS WORKS

It's a Beautiful and Powerful treasure to grow Up In a Prayer-Filled Home. From The Moment the children are Conceived Until They Reach Adulthood, Parents always Pray for them. Children Can Learn to Pray To The Lord With Their Parents, and they also teach their children the same. Siblings Can Pray For And Alongside One Another. As they Work Through Disagreements

And Create Strong Bonds. During Both Joyful And Difficult Seasons, Extended Family May Cover Loved Ones in Prayer.

We Frequently Pray For Broad Breakthroughs And Then Wait For Anything To Happen. We Never Consider Asking For The Exact Breakthroughs That We Require from the Lord, especially when we have to pray for our parents. To some people, it can be challenging to Know how To Pray For, what to pray for, or What To ask for in prayer. One Of The Most Straightforward Methods to correct this is to Pray God's Word Back To Him. When We Accomplish This, Our Wants And Perceptions Become Aligned With His, Resulting in a Spiritual Breakthrough prayer.

For Example, we are so convinced that The Lord Is At Work In all of us. Our strength comes from praying for each other. Praying for all our parents and their friends is essential because they all took part in our well-being physically and spiritually while we were young, and now as they get weaker in strength and health even in mind and Heart, general Life lets stand by them too. We are confident that their Breakthrough answers are on the Way And That all they need from the Lord will be Restored. We Believe That Believing In A Breakthrough Is Just As Crucial As Praying For It. From There, We Must Pay Great Attention And Walk-In Accordance With What We Are Informed About the impending Breakthrough.

"Keep Asking, And You Will Receive What You Ask For," Matthew 7:7-8 (NLT). Continue To Look, And You Will Find. Continue To Knock, And The Door Will Be Opened For You. Everyone Who Seeks Will Find. Everyone Who Searches Discovers. And The Door Will Be Unlocked For Anyone Who Knocks." As a result, we must Specifically Request The Breakthrough That We Require for our loved ones.

CHAPTER 3

1.1 Prayer For Parent Health

Gracious Father, Compassionately Care For our frail parents, for any in a hospice, hospital, care home, or their homes. Provide For Our parents' necessities that are beyond our understanding. Father in heaven, you Are Our Strength, And It Is Only In You That We May Discover True Inner Peace And Contentment. Please Tenderly Care For our Parents' Health And Offer Them Enough Strength To Meet Their Physical Problems. As They Battle With Their Old Bodies. Allow Your Serenity And Happiness To Rest On Them, Keeping Their Minds And Hearts Peaceful And Sustaining Their Lives And Health. In Jesus' Name, Amen.

Dear Lord, All our Parents and guardians, Bless Them And Keep Them In Your Care. May your Peace, Health, And Healing Be With Them. Reward Them For Their selflessness to bring us up, faith, loyalty, efforts, and goodness.

Lord repay them for all Their Love And Thoughtfulness, Their Presents And Prayers. Give Them A Long And Happy Marriage. May They Reach Old Age In The Presence Of Family And Friends. And When Life Is Done, reunite them In

The Kingdom Of Your Love, Where There Will Be No More Parting.

We Ask This Through Christ Our Lord. Amen

Father, In Jesus' Name, we Intercede On Behalf Of All Parents Who Worked Hard to see their children succeed, Maintaining Integrity, And diligence Got Elderly In The Service Of The Almighty. May God Provide Them With The Ability To Reap The Benefits Of Their Remaining Strength, Share The Treasure Of Their Knowledge And Wisdom, And Enter His Kingdom At The End Of Their Earthly Life.

Amen.

Prayer point

Lord, May This Tidal Surge Of Strength, Power, And Love Wash Over our Lovely parent/s And heal them.

O Lord, May This Tide Wash Away The Illness And Heal Them of all Wounds And Pain.

Holy Spirit intervenes when all human knowledge has failed. O Lord, So That our parents May Dwell and May Soak In Your Redeeming Power.

Take our parents' Hands, Lord, And Help them To Be More Of You. Comfort them In This Hour. In Jesus Name

Amen.

Parents' Long Life prayer

Lord God, Grant Our Parents' Long Life, Happiness, And Health.

May They Remain Steadfast In Your Love And Serve As Live Reminders Of Your Presence To Their Children And Grandkids.

We Make Our Request In The Name Of Jesus Christ, Our Lord. Amen.

Father, we Know That Our Times Are In Your Hands And That There Is A Season For Everything, And we Know, Lord, That Life Does Not Continue Endlessly, But I Do Ask That she/him will Be Restored To Full Health.

Be With Them, Lord, And May they Sense Your Presence With them. We trust That Lord Will Provide For All Of our parent/s Needs And That The Physicians Will Find The Correct Medications To Aid In their speedy Recovery. Keep our parent/s or guardians In Your Loving Arms, And May they Find Rest In You, Especially During This Time Of Illness. In Jesus' Name, we pray.

Amen.

Gratitude

Thank You For The gift of parents and guardians. Indeed the saying that a parent is like our Angles on earth is true. Our parents have been great examples growing up. They Have Been there Throughout our Life. A Godly parent Who Love Jesus First And Foremost And For The Unique Way they Tenderly, Gently, Nudge their children To Turn To You Lord In All Of our Life's Circumstances.

Dear Father, Please Accept our Gratitude For Bringing parents and guardians Into our Life. Thank You For The Opportunity To Learn So Much From them, For their Grasp of The Scriptures And for their Delight In Turning To You In Prayer Daily.

Lord, As our parent/s and guardians grow, we trust That You Will Wrap Your Loving Arms Around them And Keep them Safe. Guard And Lead our parents, Defend them And Provide Everything they may Require. Bring them Increasingly Closer To You. In The Name Of Jesus, Amen.

Please, Heavenly Father, Heal our Parents And all their Illnesses And Give them All The Strength And Courage they Need To Continue To Believe In You And Keep them Around For A Little While Longer. We offer you complete authority to care for our parents and all family members during our current life challenges and make us think there is still hope. Amen

Prayer Point

Dear God,

Thank You For Giving Us Another Day To Live. May You Pardon Us For All Of Our Sins And Shower Us With Even More Benefits. Health And Long Lives. So That I Could Repay What I Owed Them. Please Enlighten Their Hearts, Brains, And Souls To The Fact That The Gift Of Long Life Is More Valuable Than Everything Else In The World.

And we Pray That You Would Lead Us To Heaven With You. In Jesus' Name, Amen.

1.2 Praying For Those That Are Struggling

Parenthood's Challenges Can Be Daunting And Perplexing At Times. It Is Critical To Pray For our Parents. We, who are now parents, can understand or Recall Those powerful moments, When we are praying for our children, Prayers For Wisdom ,etc And Assistance Battered Heaven's Gates Daily. In trying Times, When Nothing Seems Normal And So Many Families Are Fighting To Get By, we are Convinced Even More Of The Importance Of

Prayer. Do You Feel The Same Way? Our Children Require Prayer Protection, But We, As Parents, Also Require God's Assistance. We Still Approach God's Throne With Passion And Urgency, Whether In Good Or Bad Circumstances, And My Pleas Now Include Grandkids.

Prayer Can Take Flight And Fly Where We Cannot. And God Hears Us When We Pray For Our parents, grandparents ,Children Or Grandchildren. God Adores Children!

Dear Lord, we come to you as children, With Hearts Eager To Please you, In Need Of Guidance and that of our parents. We are Ready To Follow Your Lead. Many of our parents are Facing A New Normal, And they are afraid And battling to Survive. Provide our parents with the tools they need to Face The Challenges Of Motherhood/fatherhood, Especially In Difficult Times. Help our parents deal With Stress In a Calm Manner And Make Sensible Decisions Every Day. Bless those You Entrust To Our parents to Care for our parents.

Give Our parents And Guardians Eyes To See You, Hearts To Adore You, Arms To Reach Out To Others, And Legs To Run Rapidly To Do Your Will. Keep our parents away From Temptation And Set Godly Friends In Their Path To Influence Them For The Better.

Grant Wisdom And Protection for our Parents

Heavenly Father. Give our parents Wisdom, A Strong Conscience, And Protection Against Harm. Keep Evil At Bay–At All Times, But Particularly Now. Wrap Them In A Spirit Of Preparedness And Obedience, Unafraid To Stand Up For You, Even If It Means Standing Alone. Show Them–And Us–How To Make Good Use Of Our Time.

Reveal Your Purpose, Joy, And Beauty to our parents

Let Them Know That Heaven Is Their True Home, But Show Them The Beauty Of All You Have Created While They Are Still On Earth. May They Discover Purpose, Meaning, And Delight. In The Small And Large Ways That You Offer Right Now. Protect Them From Wrong Motives, Lies, And Philosophies That May Appear To Be Correct But Will Only Lead Them Away From You. Fill Them With Yourself To The Point Where They Overflow With The Character Of Christ At Every Turn.

Help our parents Offer Grace, Love, And Forgiveness.

We pray for our Parents /guardians And Grandparents; Help them guide children on the right road, and teach them that Greatness And Success are Found In Servanthood, Kindness, And Godly Character, Not In Performance. Help them shower their grandchildren With Grace; In The Same Way, You Have Showered It On Us. Let Our Love For Them Be Unconditional, Like Yours, Full Of Forgiveness While Being fruitful And Uncompromising In Teaching What Is Proper.

Make our parents Steadfast, Immovable, And Faithful In their Prayers For Them At All Times In Their Lives And Ours. When We–Or They–Make Mistakes, May We Both Go To You To Remedy Those Faults, Receive Your Mercy, And Never Give Up On This Spiritual Path With You.

Help our parents Give Assurance And Comfort.

May, our Parents, Be Slow To Rage, Quick To Listen, And Eager To Accept Our Children And great Grandkids. As The Priceless Treasures That They Are. They Need Our Assurances Of Love And Comfort Now More Than Ever. They are All Exhausted As A Result Of The Additional Stresses In Our Life. Assist our parents In Listening To Their Concerns And Disappointments. Show our parents How To be Encouraged and strong And Assist Them In Finding Innovative Ways To Use Their Time And Talents. Show our parents – And Our grand Children – How To Exhibit Concern And Love For Others During This Pandemic.

We Understand They Are Simply Gifts On Loan To Us, So We Release Them To Your Care While Never Abdicating The Responsibility You Handed To our parents To Take Excellent Care Of Them No Matter What.

Thank You For The Opportunity To have Parents, Grandparents, and guardians.

Thank You For Bestowing The Duty And Privilege Of Parenting And Grandparenting On our parents. They May Feel Helpless At Times, But You Are Powerful. They Will Find A Way Out Of This.

You Are Our Model, Lord

Lord, You Are Our parents' Example, Guide, And Only Hope. Keep them Loyal In All Circumstances, And May Our Prayers Be A Daily Covering For These Lovely Ones.

CHAPTER 4

PRAY AGAINST THEIR ENEMIES

Household Adversaries Are Similar To Armed Robbers Who Are Well-Versed In Your Possessions. It Is Extremely Difficult For Someone Who Does Not Know You Well To Operate Against You Successfully. They Are Aware Of Your Aspirations And Your Mission On This Planet.

They Can Forecast You And Will Be Correct. They Can Sometimes Become A Powerful Evil From Which No One Can Escape. These Evil

Forces Can Take the Form Of Your Father, Mother, Siblings, Cousins, Relatives, Neighbours, Or Landlord through Dreams. The Devil Can Easily Possess Their Features Or Pictures And Use Them Against You.

Except For Supernatural Intervention, Their Operation Is Always A Success. In The Instance Of Joseph, His Brethren (Household) Despised Him Because His Father Jacob Adored Him. Also, His Coat Of Many Colours Was A Declaration Of His Dreams, Destiny, And Future. "Woe To The Bloody City!" Cries Nahum 3:1. It's All Lies And Robbery; The Prey Does Not Flee." That Is, The Wicked Will Be Cursed.

Another Item To Emphasize Here Is That These Household Adversaries Steal, Kill, And Destroy With The Help Of Satanic Spirits. The Domestic Onslaught Is A Continuous Spiritual Assault. Its Powers Are Harsher To Their Victims, But With The Power Of Jesus' Name, They Bow And Surrender. On The Other Hand, Household Adversaries Are Incredibly Cunning And have Know-How To Enter Their Victims. Judas Iscariot, One Of The Twelve Disciples Who Ate, Sang,

Danced, Healed, And Preached Beside Jesus, Willingly Gave Him Over To His Enemies.

Household Enemies Causing our parents And Family Grief Die By Fire In The Name Of Jesus.

Household Powers That Have Pledged To Return our parents to Square One are destroyed now In The Name Of Jesus.

Household Wickedness Powers Tasked With Destroying our parents' Life Perish In The Name Of Jesus.

In Jesus' Name, Let Every Evil Hand Of Unrepentant Household Wickedness On our parents' Life Catch Fire.

In Jesus' Name, Eliminate Any Domestic Authorities Engaged In Witchcraft operations for our parents' Sake.

In The Name Of Jesus, we Eliminate every Power That Cuts Off our parents' Expectations whenever Wonderful Things Come Near our parents, Thanks To The Power In Jesus' Blood.

Any Wicked Strongman In our parents' Family Who Has Sold Off our parents' Qualities For Their Gain, we Call Devastation Into Your Life And Demand The Recovery Of our parents' Virtues In Jesus' Name.

Any Wicked person Who Is Working Against our parents' Great Breakthroughs Should Repent by Thunder In Jesus' Name.

In The Name Of Jesus, Release our parents From Every Power Designed To Ruin our parents Because Of The Wickedness Of our parents' Forefathers' sins.

Every Terrible Burden That Household Wickedness Has Held In Place In our parents' Life, Shattered By Fire, In Jesus' Name.

By The Power Of Jesus' Blood, We Declare That Powers Ridiculing our parents Will Gather To Celebrate our parents This Year In Jesus' Name.

In The Name Of Jesus, Unlock Every Good Door In our parents' Life That Has Been Closed By Household Adversaries' Forces.

Every Power That Counter-Attacks, Regroups and Reinforces against our parents As A Result Of our parents' prayers are Consumed By Fire And Perish In The Name Of Jesus.

We release our parents From any Difficulties Stemming From Parental forefathers' Immorality, In Jesus' Name;

Every Authority That Does Not Want our parents To Lift their Head Die By Fire In Jesus' Name.

In Jesus' Name, Swallow Every Evil Pit Prepared For our parents By Domestic Wickedness Powers.

We command Every Polygamous Witchcraft In our parents' Family, which has been assigned to Manipulate their Glory And Exchange their Stars; In Jesus' Name, Get The Arrow Of Death.

The Spirit Of Marital Wickedness, Which Is Defiling Marriages In our parents' Family, we Arrest You Today, Die By Fire, In The Name Of Jesus.

The Spirit Of Marital Wickedness, Which Is Defiling Marriages In our parents' Family, we

Arrest You Today, Die By Fire, In The Name Of Jesus.

CHAPTER 5

PRAY GOD TO SEND THEM HELPERS

There Are Numerous Examples In Scripture That Attest To God's Assistance To Humanity. The Scriptures Below Will Encourage our parents To Keep Looking For More Verses About God's Help, As Well As To See That God Is The Ultimate Helper In their Life. Psalm 116:1-2

I Love The LORD Because He Hears My Voice And Responds To My Plea For Mercy. I'll Pray As Long As I Have Breath Because He Leans Down To Listen.

Psalm 116:1-2, David Begs God For Assistance. Not Only Do We Find A Desperate Prayer, But We Also Find God Bending Down To Listen To Him. God is Listening To Our Pleading For Assistance. It Is Revealed Later In The Psalm That God Does Deliver David From Death And Despair Because David Cried Out, And The Lord Heard Him.

Allow This Scripture To Encourage You; That God Is Listening To our parents' Requests For Assistance And That He Will Show Kindness amid Of Adversity. Isaiah 41:10,13

'Do Not be Afraid, For I Am With You; Do Not Be Discouraged, For I Am Your God.' I Will Fortify You, Yes, I Will Assist You, And I Will Uphold You With My Righteous Right Hand For I, The LORD Your

God, Will Take Your Right Hand In Mine And Say To You, 'Do Not Be Afraid; I Will Help You.'

This Scripture Encourages God's People To Be Steady In Their Belief That God Is Their Helper And Savior. When We Set Our Gaze On The Truth That God Will Support Us In Times Of Need And Adversity, We Have Nothing To Fear. God Promises That He Would Supply Even In The Most Severe Of Circumstances. In Verse 17, The Lord Says, "When The Poor And Needy Seek Water, And There Is None, And Their Tongues Are Parch From Thirst, Then I, The LORD, Will Answer Them." "I, The God Of Israel, Will Never Leave Them."

"Because You Have Been My Help, I Will Rejoice In The Shadow Of Your Wings."

— Psalm 63:7

This Verse Bears Witness To God's Assistance To David. David Had A Perilous Life, Filled With Suffering And Strife. However, Because David

Records An Account Of God's Help, We Might Be Encouraged To Know That God Is Faithful Even amid Adversity.

Prayer Point

Loving Heavenly Father, You Created All Things, And All Things Are Held Together By Your Might. We Beseech You, Lord, To Help our parents Get Through This Difficult Moment In their Lives, According To Your Abundant Mercy.

Lord, You Know parents Have Troubles at Home And In The Family, As Well As Financial And Relational Issues, All Of Which Seem To Have Hit struck our parents Hard At The Same Moment. Our parents Don't Know What To Do, Lord, But they keep their eyes on you. Strengthen our parents With Your Force, And Assist our parents To Focus On You Rather Than their Surroundings. Our parents Know Your Grace Is Adequate Because Your Strength Is Made Perfect In their Weakness.

Lord, We Know That You Are Capable Of Doing The Impossible In Our parents' Lives And That

You Are Capable Of Doing Far More Than We Can Ask Or Dream. We Cast All Of our parents' Worries On You, For You Have Promised To Carry them And Help them In the Hour Of their Need. In Jesus' Name, We ask You For Assistance.

Amen.

Jesus, Lord, we Beseech You To Hear Their Request, For They Are Weak And Defenceless, With No One To Turn To In Times Of Trouble But You. They Are Completely Lost And Alone, With No Idea Where To Turn. Their Bodies Have Become So Feeble, Their Eyes Have Turned Red With Tears, And Things Have Become So Difficult That I Beg You To Grant Them Your Kindness.

Keep Them From Going Under And Giving Up, I Pray. You Are My God, And I Have Put My Trust In You. Lord, You Have Promised To Be With

Them In Their Times Of Need And To Carry Them When Circumstances Get Too Difficult. You Have Promised To Transport Them, And I Am Requesting Your Assistance.

Lord, our parents are Your Servants And Have always Trusted You. We Beseech You To Come To Their Help In Their Hour Of Need And To Carry Them In Your Loving Arms. All Day Long, They Lift Their Hearts To You, Lord, And Trust You To Help Them As You Have Promised. In Jesus' Name, we pray, Amen.

Chapter 6

Pray For God's Protection For Them

Honouring Parents Entails More Than Just Giving Cards On Important Occasions. And It's More Than Just A Dinner Invitation Now And Then.

In The Biblical Context (Exodus 20:12; Ephesians 6:2), It Comprises Respect And A Commitment On The Part Of Grown Children To Care For Their Parents, Particularly When They Are Ill. It Is A

Magnificent Manifestation Of The Gospel. God Loves Us all as His Children, And He Exemplifies a Constant, Caring Ministry.

Prayer Point

Father we are Grateful That our Parents Trust In You. We are Aware That There Are Many Parents ,guardians And Elderly Loved Ones Who Do Not Know You yet, Lord, we Pray and ask You To Woo Them To Yourself And Bring About Their Redemption And Change (Ephesians 2:8-9; 2 Timothy 1:9; 2 Peter 3:9).

We Pray That You May Recall To our Loved Ones All The Ways You Have Been Their Hope And Help—In Many Cases, From Childhood (Psalm 62:5; 71:5; 121:2).

We are Grateful For All The Ways. You Used our Parents To Influence our Childhood. What A Priceless Present! our Parents have Helped us In Practical Ways And taught us To trust You. Although our Parents Were Not Perfect, we Could Sense Their Desire To Shape us Into Good

People, And we are so Grateful we were Encouraged To Become Christians.

The Roles Have Now Been Flipped. We Have The Honour Of Assisting And Serving, As Well As Reminding our Loved One Of Your Compassionate, Shepherding Care. Give us Patience, Insight, And A Kind Heart. Please Help us To Continue To Express Respect And Appreciation, As Well As To Value Who You, In Your Providence, Made our Loved One Be (Exodus 20:12)

Finally, we Know Your Concern For our Parents Exceeds Anything we Can Offer Because Every Wonderful Gift Comes From You .Jamcs 1:17.

PARENT'S PROTECTION.

We Pray That our Parents Will Continue To Rely On You, The Rock Of Strength And Righteousness (Psalm 71:3a; 73:26; 92:12-15). Spread Your Protection Over our Parents, For You Are The Ultimate Refuge .Psalm 5:11; 46:1.

We ask You To Keep our Parents Safe From The Wicked One And To Show Them The Way Out When They Are Tempted (2 Thessalonians 3:3; 1 Corinthians 10:13). Every Day, May Wisdom, Discernment, And Knowledge Safeguard And Lead our parents (Proverbs 4:6; 2:11; 138:7).

We Pray that our Parents Would Be Brave And Confident In Your Presence, Assistance, And Deliverance (Psalm 121:1-8; Deuteronomy 31:6; Isaiah 41:10; Psalm 34:19; Psalm 91).

Verses Of Protection:

1. "He Who Dwells In The Shadow Of The Almighty Will Rest In The Shelter Of The Highest." "He Is My Refuge And My Fortress, My God, In Whom I Put My Trust," I Shall Say About The Lord. He Will Cover You With His Feathers, And You Will Find Refuge Under His Wings; His Loyalty Will Be Your Shield And Rampart... He Will Direct His Angels To Protect You In All Your Endeavours. I Will Save Those Who Love Me, And I Will Defend Those Who Call On My Name..." Psalm 91:1-2, 4, 11, 14, 15
2. "Fear Not, For I Am With You; Be Not Frightened, For I Am Your God." I Will Help You And Strengthen You; I Will Sustain You With My Righteous Right Hand." 41:10 (Isaiah)

3. "The Lord Will Keep An Eye On Your Comings And Goings Both Now And Forever." 121:8 Psalm

4. "The Lord's Name Is A Sturdy Tower; The Righteous Run Into It And Is Safe." 18:10 Proverbs

5. "But The Lord Is Faithful, And He Will Strengthen And Safeguard You From The Evil One," Says Verse 5. 3rd Thessalonians 3:3.

6. "For God Has Not Given Us A Spirit Of Fear, But Of Power, Love, And A Clear Mind," Says Verse 6. 2 Timothy 1:7 (KJV).

7. "Because He Has Stated, "I Will Never Leave You Nor Forsake You." So We May Confidently Declare, "The Lord Is My Helper; I Will Not Be Afraid." "What Is A Man Capable Of Doing To Me?" 5–6 (Hebrews 13:5–6)

8. "My God Is My Refuge, My Shield, And The Horn Of My Salvation." He Is My Fortress, My

Sanctuary, And My Savior; You Deliver Me From The Clutches Of Violent Men. I Cry Out To The Lord, Who Is Deserving Of Honour, And I Am Delivered From My Adversaries." 2 Samuel 22:3-4 (KJV).

9. "You Are My Refuge; You Will Keep Me Safe; You Will Surround Me With Songs Of Deliverance." 10. Psalm 32:7 "I Shall Lie Down And Sleep Peacefully Because You Alone, O Lord, Help Me Dwell In Safety." 4:8 Psalm

10. "The Lord Bless You And Keep You, The Lord Make His Face Shine On You And Be Gracious To You, The Lord Turn His Face Toward You And Give You Peace," Says The Lord. (Numbers 6:24–26)

11. "The Fear Of The Lord Brings Life, And Whoever Has It Is Content; He Will Not Be Visited By Evil." 19:23 (Proverbs)

12. "Even If I Have To Travel Down The Darkest Valley, I Will Not Be Afraid Since You Are Beside Me..." 23:4 (Psalm)
13. "...No Weapon Used Against You Will Be Successful." You Will Silence Every Accusatory Voice Raised Against You." Isaiah 54:17 (KJV).
14. "God Is Our Refuge And Strength, A Very Present Help In Trouble," Says The Bible. Psalm 46:1 (KJV)

Chapter 7

Pray For Their Investment

Work Ethics, According To The Bible, Begins at Home. What We Teach Our Children About Work, Such As Attendance, Punctuality, And Working As Though For The Lord, Has A Huge Impact On The Type Of Employees Or Even Company Leaders They Will Be In The Future.

"Leave Your Children On The Correct Path, And They Will Not Stray When They Are Older." -

Psalms 22:6 (NLT) Our parents have shown us the way .

Prayer Point

Please Hear Our Prayers, Lord Jesus . Our Father assist our parents Family's Business that Has Been Struggling, And We Urgently Require Your Assistance.

Please Give Favourable Possibilities to our parents That Will Benefit them and all their loved ones. Keep our parents Safe From Anyone Or Anything That Will Be A Burden To Our Family And Business. Please Assist Us In Rebuilding Our Business So That It Can Once Again Be Successful, Lucrative, And Give Financial Abundance.

May our parents Always Be Able To Provide For their Families And Employees In This Abundance. Assist our parents In Making Sound Decisions And Guiding Us. We Request That our parents Be

Paid In Full For All Money Owed To them For Work That they Have Done In Good Faith.

Father May our parents be Able To Pay Off All Off their Debts That Have Been Bothering them. Please Grant That they Survive All Of These Trials And Tribulations.

Allow our parents Family's Business To Be Prosperous And Successful Once More. Thank You For Listening To Our Petitions, And Please Bless Our Family And Business With Much-Needed Financial Wealth And Prosperity.In Jesus' Name Amen.

Bible Verses About Business

1. "God Rewards Those Who Give Generously And Conduct Themselves Fairly." Psalm 112:5.
2. "You Have Six Days Each Week For Regular Work, But You Must Stop Working On The Seventh Day." This Allows Your Ox And Donkey Time To Rest. It Also Refreshes The Slaves And Foreigners Who Live Among You." -Exodus 23:12 (KJV)
3. "The Lord Has Endowed Them With Exceptional Abilities As Engravers, Designers, Embroiderers In A Blue, Purple, And Scarlet Thread On Fine Linen Cloth, And Weavers." They Are Skilled Artisans And Designers." Exodus 35:35.
4. "Do Not Defraud Or Rob A Neighbour." Do Not Make Your Hired Staff Wait Until The Next Day To Be Paid." -See Leviticus 19:13.

5. "When Weighing Items, You Must Use Accurate Scales And Full And Honest Measures." Yes, Always Use Accurate Weights And Measures So That You Can Live A Long And Prosperous Life In The Country That The Lord Your God Has Given You." – Deuteronomy 25:13–15 (NLT).
6. "How Could I Face God If I Had Been Unjust To My Male Or Female Servants When They Presented Their Grievances To Me?" "What Could I Say When He Interrogated Me?" - Proverbs 31:13-14 (NLT).
7. "Lazy People Become Poor Quickly, But Dedicated Workers Become Wealthy." -Psalms 10:4 (NLT).
8. "The Lord Despises The Use Of Dishonest Scales, But He Delights In Exact Weights." Proverbs 11:1 (NLT).

9. "Those Who Work Hard Will Prosper, While Those Who Are Lazy Will Prosper." -Psalms 13:4 (NLT).
10. "Wealth From Get-Rich-Quick Schemes Vanishes Quickly, But Wealth From Hard Work Grows Over Time." Proverbs13:11.

CHAPTER 8

PRAY FOR THEIR PENSION

Though A Full-Time Job Eventually Ends, There Is No Such Thing As Retirement In The Christian Life.

The Bible Is Full Of Tales Of Older Men And Women Who Were Miraculously Used By God Simply Because They Were Willing To Be Used.

It Comes As No Surprise. For Many People, The Stage Known As "Retirement" Provides More Time And Fewer Interruptions. Our parents have Accumulated A Tremendous Bank Of Experience, And If they've Walked Diligently With The Lord For Any Period Of Time, they've Collected Invaluable Wisdom And Important Spiritual Truths.

Consider The Influence God Can Have In The Lives Of Others Through You!

For Christians, Retirement Should Be About More Than Exotic Vacations, Golf Games, And Daytime Television (Though None Of Those Things Is Improper In Moderation).

It Should Always Be About Two Things In The Christian Life: Divine Contact And Faithful Stewardship.

Not Emphasizing My Comfort, But Emphasizing His Kindness.

Not For our Own Enjoyment, But To Bring Him Praise.

Pursuing Him rather than our Ideas.

Consider Confiding In God Through The Practice Of Praying The Scriptures If You Want To Get Closer To Him And Are Willing To Be A Tool In His Hand At This Season Of our parents Life.

Prayer Point

Dear Father God, Thank You For The Seasons Of Life, For The Joy Of Childhood, The Thrill Of Adolescence, And The Security Of Age. Thank You For The Blessings That Come With Age, For All The Good Memories To Cherish, For The Wisdom That Comes With Experience, And For The Freedom That Retirement Provides especially for our parents now.

Lord, We Thank You For The Wonderful Blessing That Has Resulted From Many Years Of Hard Effort, And We Thank You That You Continue To Anoint And Use our parents always, In All Seasons.

We Pray That This Will Be A New Beginning For our parents, That their Hope Will Soar, And That their Vision Will Guide them. May A New Rhythm Arise, One That Strikes A Lovely Balance

Between Relaxation And Participation In Life. And Now, Lord, We Ask For Your Blessing upon our parents.

May This Day And Every Day After That Bring our parents Good Health, Joy In Abundance, And Serenity Of Heart And Mind. In Jesus Name,

Amen.

Claim God's Promise That He Is Able To Make All Grace Abundant To our parents, So That they May Abound In All Good Works At All Times, Having All Sufficiency In All Things At All Times (2 Corinthians 9:8).

Share Your Needs For Caring For Your Parents With Him, Confident That He Will Completely Equip You For The Excellent Task To Which He Has Called You.

Parents Are A Priceless Gift From You, Heavenly Father.

Thank You For Allowing us To Have The Pleasure Of Having our Parents For Many Decades So That we May Enjoy And Learn From Them.

Father ,We Ask That You Will Assist And Guide Them With Their Pension And Allow Them To Continue Developing In Grace And In Their Connection With You Till The End Of Their Time On Earth.

Please Give us The Wisdom And Strength To Care For Them In A Way That Honours Both Them And You. We Pray In The Name Of My Lord And Savior, Jesus Christ. Amen.

Pray To God To Help You Honour Your Father And Mother For The Rest Of Your Life (Exodus 20:12). Ask Him To Assist You In Treating Your Parents With Respect, Not Rebuking Them But

Encouraging Them From The Bottom Of Your Heart (I Timothy 5:1-2).

Commit Your Desire To Care For Your Parents To The Lord In Any Way He Sees Fit. Ask Him To Help You Demonstrate Godliness To Them By Repaying A Portion Of All They've Done For You, As This Is Pleasant In God's Sight (I Timothy 5:4).

Dear Heavenly Father, Thank You For A Season Of Relaxation After My Parents' Years Of Hard And Fruitful Effort. We Pray That You Will Help Them Remember That There Is No Such Thing As Retiring From Your Ministry As Long As They Are Living On This Earth. Keep In Mind The Responsibility They Have For Properly Stewarding The Time, Talents, And Riches You Have Given Them. May They Constantly Use

Them For Your Glory. We Pray In The Name Of My Lord And Savior, Jesus Christ. Amen.

Chapter 9

Pray For Parents Not To Lack

When we were young, Some Of Us Moved Away From Home. We Graduated And Went Off In Quest Of Careers And Futures, Which Separated Us From Our Parents.

Calls And Facetime Keep Us In Touch, But It's Not The Same For Our Parents. We May Pay Them A Visit On Holidays And Vacations, But Not As Frequently As They Would Want.

The Love We Have For Our Parents Has Not Changed, Only Our Situations In Life.

As Time Goes On, We Find Ourselves In The Roles Of Adults And Parents. Hopefully, We Will Continue To Practice Daily Prayer And Pass It Down To The Next Generation Of Children.

However, The Prayers We Prayed As Children Gave Way To Those Centred On Our Children, Careers, And The Demands Of Our Busy Life. We Pray For Ourselves As Well As For Future Generations.

But What About Our Parents And Grandparents? Do You Ever Pause To Say A Prayer For Your Parents?

As Time Passes, Our Parents Are Subjected To Changes Over Which They Have Little Control. Where They Once Occupied A Prominent Position In Our Lives, They Now Observe Us From The Sidelines. They Encourage Us While Succumbing To The Ravages Of Time.

They May Conceal Their Issues In Order Not To Disrupt Their Children's Lives. They Only Care About What Is Best For Them, Even If It Means Jeopardizing Their Own Health And Safety.

Before We All Become Depressed By These Ideas, We Must Realize That This Is A Normal Part Of Life's Cycle. Children Grew Up And Left Their Parents Even In Biblical Times.

Our Goal Here Is To Remind Each Of Us Of The Sacrifices Our Parents Made So That We Could Live Our Lives. As Part Of That Responsibility, We Must Ensure That We Pray For Them As Well.

Life Continues To Move Us Forward, But We Must Take Time To Reflect. Praise Your Parents By Praying For Them On A Daily Basis. Prayer Is A Fantastic Technique To Arm Yourself Spiritually.

Prayer Point

Dear Father, In Your Lovely Book Of Psalms103:17, You Give Us This Magnificent Promise: "From Eternal To Everlasting, The Lord's Love Is With Those Who Fear Him, And His Righteousness With Their Children's Children." What Better Promise Could You Make To our parents Than To See their Children And Their Offspring Blessed With Your Love And Righteousness?

We Also Ask For Your Hand Of Blessing To Be On Us. Bless Us With The Strength To Be There For Those We Care About, As Well As The Knowledge To Know What To Say To Convey Comfort, Encouragement, And Sometimes Unpleasant Truth. We Will Require Your Patience As We Await Your Perfect Will And Way In The

Lives Of Each Of Our Loved Ones. Lord God, We Are Eternally Grateful. Amen.

Father In Heaven, It's Difficult For us To See our parents Slow Down As They Get Older. Thank You For Your Generosity In Providing Parents And Relatives. Thank You For All Of The Time we Get To Spend With Them And Everything They've Taught us Over The Years.

Strengthen Them Both Mentally And Physically. Make Provisions For Their Needs. Allow Them To Continue Walking In Grace With You And Growing In Your Wisdom.

Please Help us To Comprehend Their Needs And To Have The Insight To Know What To Do For Them. Teach us To Respect our Parents Today And Always, And Help us To Provide A Good Example For our Children To Follow.

Allow Your Comfort And Love To Fill Their Final Days. We Pray In Jesus' Name. Amen.

You Fed The Hungry, Lord Jesus, And You Shared Your Bread With All.

Your People Are Hungry Right Now, And We Are Called To Share Their Bread.

May Rains Fall On The Dry And Broken Ground, Quenching Your People's Hunger And Causing Seeds To Grow Tall And Flourish, Yielding A Plentiful Harvest.

May We Share The Gifts You Bestow Upon our parents And Bring Solace To Those In Need. May We Demonstrate Love Via Our Deeds So That Everyone Has Enough To Eat.

We Pray In The Name Of Jesus Christ, Our Lord. Amen.

Bible References

The Earth Is The Lord's And All That Is In It, The World, And Those Who Live In It; (Psalm 24:1)

God Visits The Earth And Waters It, Greatly Enriching The Earth…. Softening It With Showers And Blessing Its Growth.

God Provides The People With Grain.

God Grants Peace Within Your Borders;

God Fills You With The Finest Of Wheat. (Psalm 147:14)

The Lord Watches Over The Strangers;

God Upholds The Orphan And The Widow, But The Way Of The Wicked, God Brings To Ruin. (Psalm 146:9)

O Give Thanks To The Lord, For God Is Good;

God's Steadfast Love Endures Forever! (Psalm 118:1)

O Lord, Who May Abide In Your Tent?

Who May Dwell On Your Holy Hill? (Psalm 15:1)

CHAPTER 10

WHAT DOES THE BIBLE SAY ABOUT CARING FOR OUR PARENTS?

Where Did You Learn To Pray? Many Of Us Learned About Prayers From Our Parents As They Tucked Us Into Bed Each Night. Maybe They Taught You This Simple Prayer: "Now I Lay Me Down To Sleep; I Pray The Lord To Keep My Soul."

May God Keep Me Safe Through The Night And Awaken Me With The Light Of The Morning, Amen."

They Deepened Our Understanding Of The Significance Of Spending Time Each Day With God.

Here Are Some Verses About Parents And Aging To Consider:

- Exodus 20:12 Says, "Honor Your Father And Mother So That You May Live A Long Time In The Land That The LORD Your God Is Giving You."
- Isaiah 46:4: "I Am He Who Will Sustain You Even In Your Old Age And Grey Hairs." I Created You, And I Will Carry You, Sustain You, And Rescue You."
- 1 Timothy 5:1-2 States, "Do Not Rebuke An Older Man Harshly, But Exhort Him As If

He Were Your Father." With Absolute Purity, Treat Younger Men As Brothers; Older Women As Mothers; And Younger Women As Sisters."

- Leviticus 19:32 Says, "Stand Up In The Presence Of The Aged, Respect The Elderly, And Revere Your God." "My Name Is The Lord."

- 1 Peter 5:1: "I Appeal To The Elders Among You As A Fellow Elder And A Witness Of Christ's Sufferings, Who Will Also Share In The Glory To Be Revealed."

- Psalm 71:9: "Do Not Abandon Me When I Am Old; Do Not Abandon Me When My Strength Is Gone."

- 1 Timothy 5:8 Says, "But Whoever Does Not Provide For His Own, Especially For Those In His Household, Has Denied The Faith And Is Worse Than An Unbeliever."

- 1 Timothy 5:4: "But If A Widow Has Children Or Grandchildren, Let Them First Learn To Show Godliness To Their Own Household And To Return Some To Their Parents, For This Is Pleasing In God's Sight."
- Even As We Grow Older, God Is Concerned About Us. And When God Is Concerned About Something, We Are Called To Be Concerned As Well. Don't Forget To Remember Your Parents In Your Prayers. Recognize That As They Age, They Will Require Your Assistance In A Variety Of Ways.

Here Are Some Ways To Show Your Parents You Care During Their Golden Years:

- Contact Them As Frequently As Possible.
- Pay Attention To Them And Emphasize What They Say.
- Speak Up For Their Care And Needs.
- If You Are Unable To Visit, Ask Others To Assist You Around The House With Tasks Such As Mowing Or Cleaning.
- Motivate Them To Stay Active.
- Make Memories By Doing Activities Together.
- Be Encouraging Without Being Bossy.
- Send Greeting Cards And Drawings Created By Their Grandchildren.

If You Still Have your parents, Cherish Them Because They Will Be Gone One Day. Now Is The Time To Do Everything You Can To Help Them.

Set A Good Example For Your Children So That They Will Know How To Look After You In The Future. Growing Old Is A Gift From God, And It Is Our Responsibility To Make Those Final Years As Enjoyable As Possible.

Scriptures To Pray Over Your Family

"The Lord Bless You And Keep You; The Lord Make His Face Shine On You And Be Gracious To You; The Lord Turn His Face Toward You And Give You Peace," Says Numbers 6:24-26.

Please Bless My Family And Children, Lord. Give Them Hearts That Will Follow You.

"Do Not Be Afraid Or Terrified Because Of Them, For The Lord Your God Goes With You; He Will Never Leave You Nor Forsake You," Deuteronomy 31:6 Says.

Give My Family The Courage To Face Their Fears. Give Them The Strength To Stand Up For What Is Right.

"Create In Me A Clean Heart, O God, And Renew A Right Spirit Within Me," Says Psalm 51:10.

Create An Attitude Of Integrity In Them, And They Will Devote Their Lives To Bringing You Glory.

"Jesus Said, 'Behold, I Give You Authority To Trample On Serpents And Scorpions, And Over All The Power Of The Enemy And Nothing Shall By Any Means Hurt You," Says Luke 10:19.

Allow My Family To Walk Under Your Authority. May They Comprehend And Live Each Day, Asserting The Authority You Have Bestowed Upon Them As Your Children.

"Do Not Be Anxious About Anything," Philippians 4:6 Says, "But In Every Situation, By Prayer And Petition, With Thanksgiving, Present Your Requests To God."

Give Them A Spirit Of Courage And Surrender Rather Than Fear.

Prayer For Parents Or Family Hurt Each Other

Thank You, Father, For Family. You Tell Us That Being Alone Is Bad For Us, So You've Surrounded Us With People Who Have An Impact On Our Lives And Moved Us Away From The Loneliness Of Solitude. Exodus 15:2 Reminds Us That "The Lord Is My Strength And My Song." We Must Keep In Mind That Our Family Is Not Responsible For Our Happiness. They Are Not Responsible For The State Of Our Hearts And Souls. And They Cannot Control How We Feel, Nor Can They Enter Our Minds To Comprehend The Depth Of Our Emotions.

When We Are Misunderstood Or Misunderstood By A Family Member, We Feel Helpless To Argue Our Case. Help Us To Remember Exodus 15:2. You Are Our Pillar Of Strength. The Inability To

Filter Our Thoughts Is A Sign That We Should Surrender Them To You. Please Help Us To Be Patient When You Respond With Silence. Inspire Us To Remember Who You Say We Are Through The Power Of Your Holy Spirit. Loved. Forgiven. Saved. Purposeful. One-Of-A-Kind.

Thank You For Providing The Comfort Of Family. A Mother And Father's Warm Embrace, Siblings, And Extended Family. There Is Something About Being Related That Makes It Easier To Trust Other People. When And If That Trust Is Violated By Abuse And Abandonment, We Pray For Your Physical Protection As Well As Your Guardianship Over Our Hearts And Minds. Allow Us To Seek Your Assistance And Counsel, As Well As That Of Others Who Have Been Trained To Assist Us In Avoiding Danger And Harm. Anyone Who Intends To Harm Us Or Abuse Us Is

Not Someone. You Want Us To Spend Time With You.

We Confess All The Words We Wish We Could Change. Our Sinful Nature, As A Result Of Adam And Eve's Error In The Garden, Can Lead Us Down Paths We Know Are Wrong And Into Mistakes, We Had No Intention Of Making. However, Because Of Jesus' Sacrifice, We Are Forgiven Over And Over When We Confess To You In The Name Of Our Savior. Help Us To Extend The Same Compassion To Those Who Test Our Hearts And Patience. Bless Us With Patience And Wisdom, With The Desire To Seek You First And To Speak Kindness. When We Are Wrong, Convict Us And Strengthen Our Resolve To Apologize.

Hurt Within Families Has The Potential To Damage Relationships Permanently. But, With

Your Help, Anything And Everyone Can Be Restored. You Are The Healer For Us. We Find Peace In You. Our Faith Is In You. And When We Let Go And Let You Determine The Path, Our Faith Can Pull Us Across Any Divide. "When These Things Begin To Take Place," Luke Says, "Stand Up And Lift Up Your Heads, Because Your Redemption Is Near" (Luke 21:5-28). Jesus Is On His Way. That Is Without A Doubt. We Want To Follow Him Closely And Intently Until He Returns To Take Us Home Or We Return To Him In Heaven.

It's Easy To Become Bitter In The Midst Of Conflict And Pain. Miscommunication Can Provide Justification For Severing A Relationship Like A Dead Tree Branch. Payback And Comebacks Play Over And Over In Our Heads. The Cycle Of Vindication Continues Indefinitely. But God, You Tell Us To Concentrate On You

(Colossians 2:19). Allow The World To Explain Itself, But First, Allow Us To Listen To You.

God, You Are Present In Agony We Can't Bear, Don't Understand, And Want To Flee. Hold Us And Assist Us. Allow Us To Sit In Silence For Long Periods Of Time Until We Are Certain You Have Inspired Our Choice Of Words. Encourage Our Hearts To Forgive And To Pray For Those On The Other Side Of A Squabble. Bless Those Who Have Harmed Us, And Help Us To Be A Blessing In Your Name. In The Name Of Jesus, Amen.

CHAPTER 11

SCRIPTURES TO PRAY OVER YOUR FAMILY

A Prayer For Protection:

The Lord Your God, The Mighty Warrior Who Saves, Is With You. He Will Take Great Pleasure In You; In His Love, He Will No Longer Rebuke You But Will Sing Joyously Over You. NIV Zephaniah 3:17

Prayer point:

Thank You, Lord, For Always Keeping An Eye On our parents. It's Incredible That You're Singing For Joy Over Us Right Now. You Are The Valiant Warrior Who Saves The Day. This Day, May We Find Solace In Your Love.

A Prayer For Peace:

'May The Lord Bless And Keep You.' May The Lord Bless You And Keep You In His Good Graces. 'May The Lord Bless You And Keep You In His Peace.' Numbers 6:24-26

Lord, We Thank You For Being The God Of Peace. We Are Grateful That Even When The Earth Trembles, We Can Be Still And Know You Are God. Nothing Can Keep Us Apart From You. We Thank You For Your Protection And Kindness. Give our parents Your Perfect Peace As We Sit In Your Presence And Focus Our parents

Hearts And Minds On You. We Have Faith That You Will Guide our parents, Protect our parents, And Be Gracious To our parents No Matter What. Amen.

For Compassion:

And Be Useful, Helpful, And Kind To One Another, Tenderhearted (Compassionate, Understanding, Loving-Hearted), Forgiving One Another [Readily And Freely], Just As God In Christ Forgave You. Ephesians 4:32

Prayer:

Dear Heavenly Father, We Praise You For Your Unending Love. We Thank You For Allowing our parents to Love Others because Of your Love. We Ask That You Help Us To Be Kind To one another, To Show Mercy, Forgiveness, And The Love You've So Generously Shared With our parents. May We, As A Family, Be Compassionate

To One Another. Show Us Any Areas In Our Hearts Where We Need To Change Or Repent. May We Be As Willing To Forgive Our Family And Friends As You Are To Forgive Us. Amen.

For Harmony:

If Any Of our parents has a Grudge Against Someone, help them to be Patient And Forgive One Another. Forgive Just As The Lord Has Forgiven You. And Put On Love, Which Binds All These Virtues Together In Perfect Unity. Colossians 3:13-14

For Wisdom:

Don't Turn Your Back On Wisdom; She Will Guard You. If You Love Her, She Will Protect You. Obtaining Wisdom Is The Most Prudent Thing You Can Do! And, Above All, Develop Sound Judgment. NLT Proverbs 4:6-7

Prayer:

Dear God, We Thank You For Freely Giving Us Wisdom When We Ask For It. We Require Your Expertise. Because Your Ways Are Higher Than Ours, And Your Thoughts Are Higher Than Ours. You Notice Things That We Don't. Inspire Our Family's Hearts To Pursue Wisdom With Zeal. Assist Our Family In Developing Sound Judgment. Direct Our parents Steps And Give them Direction In All Aspects Of Our parents Lives. Amen.

For Encouragement:

My Flesh And Heart Fail; But God Is My Heart's Strength And My Portion Forever.　Psalm73:26 (NKJV)

Prayer:

We Thank You, Lord, For Your Tenacity. You Never Let our parents Down. You Are Our Saviour In Our Hour Of Need. This Day, God, We Give You Our parents Worries, Burdens, And Concerns. Thank You That We Never Have To Worry Because You Are Always Right Beside our parents. Today, Remind Us Of Your Goodness. We Pray In Jesus' Name. Amen.

A Prayer Concerning God's Faithfulness.

I Am Aware That The Lord Is Always With us. I'm Not Going To Be Shaken Because He's Right Beside us. Psalm 16:8

For Perseverance:

We are Aware That The Lord Is Always With our parents. I'm Not Going To Be Shaken Because He's Right Beside them. NLT Psalm 16:8

Prayer: Dear Heavenly Father, We Thank You For Always Being Right Beside our parents. We Thank You For Never Leaving them And Always Holding their Right Hands. We Pray That Your Praise Will Be On their Lips Always, In Good Times And Bad. Even If The Earth Shakes And Rainfalls, We Will Not Be Shaken Because You Are Always With us all. Remind Each Member Of Our Family Today That You Are At Our Right Hand In A Special Way.

For A Disciplined Life:

For The Time Being, No Discipline Brings Joy; Instead, It Appears Sad And Painful; However, For Those Who Have Been Trained By It, It Yields The Peaceful Fruit Of Righteousness [Right Standing With God And A Lifestyle And Attitude That Seeks Conformity To God's Will And Purpose]. AMP Hebrews 12:11

Prayer:

We Thank You, God, For The Teachable Moments. As A Family, We Pray That We Will Seek Wisdom And Live A Disciplined Life. Keep Our Hearts Safe From Temptation And Assist our parents In Carrying Out their Will And Purposes For their Lives.

For Confident Hope:

We Pray That God, The Source Of Hope, Will Completely Fill our parents With Joy And Peace .As A Result Of Your Faith In Him By The Power Of The Holy Spirit, You Will Overflow With Confident Hope. Romans 15:13

Prayer:

We Rejoice Today Because You Never Change, Lord. You Are The Same Person You Were Yesterday, Today, And Tomorrow. We Thank You That Your Holy Spirit Is Currently Filling Our Family With Unspeakable Joy And Peace That Surpasses All Comprehension. Not From This World's Peace Or Joy, But From YOU. Overflow In our parents As We Put Our Trust In You So That they May Be Filled With Confident Hope.

For Kindness:

Allow No Unwholesome Talk To Come Out Of Your Mouths, But Only What Is Useful For Building Others Up According To Their Needs So That Those Who Listen Can Benefit. NIV Ephesians 4:29

Prayer: This Day, May God Grant our parents The Ability To Speak Life To One Another. May We Be Kind To One Another And Use Our Words To Lift One Another Up. May We Be Able To Hear Each Other And Respond To Each Other With Compassionate Hearts.

Chapter 12

Godly Story About Parental Love

An Older Woman Is Sitting Behind Her Son, Rahul. He's Doing Some Office Work. He's Well-Educated And Well-Adjusted. His Work Is Extremely Demanding. In The Meantime, The Squirrel Comes And Sits At The House's Window. For The First Time, His Mother Inquired About His Son. Her Son Responded, "Mom, That's A Squirrel." For About A Half-Hour, His Mother

Asked What That Son Was, To Which He Replied, "It's A Squirrel, Mom."

When His Mother Asked Him The Same Question For The Third Time, He Replied Angrily And Frustratedly. Why Are You Asking Me The Same Question Over And Over When You Know It's A Squirrel? Mother Is In A Bad Mood. Her Throat Was Sore, But She Didn't Say Anything To Her Son. She Simply Stood Up And Apologized To Him, Calming Him Down.

She Forces Him To Sit Directly Behind Her And Tells Him A Sweet Little Boy Story, A Five-Year-Old Boy Story. That Little Boy Was Adorable And Innocent. Every Now And Then, A Bird Will Come And Sit On The House's Window. That Child Asked His Mother, "What Is That, Mom?" About 15 To 20 Times, And Each Time His Mother Answered Him Calmly And Sweetly. She

Kissed Her Child On The Back Of His Head To See His Innocence.

That Child Is Now Rahul, Who Is Well-Adjusted And Well-Educated, But He Doesn't Know How To Treat His Elderly Mother. That Person Could Be Anyone, Not Just Rahul. It Could Be Me, You, Or Anyone Else On The Planet. Who Doesn't Treat Their Parents With Care And Respect?

"MORAL"

Honour Your Father And Mother

Parents Make Numerous Sacrifices For Us And Our Future. They Weep For Us. No One Else In The World Can Love Us As Much As They Do. Even Now, They Are Concerned About You. It Is Now Your Responsibility To Care For Them In A Gentle And Loving Manner.

Do You Adore Your Parents As Much As we Do?

Conclusion

This book is written by authors who are sisters. This book is for everyone out there who loves and cherishes their parents and wishes to make them happy always. A family that prays together stays together forever. Prayer is a vital part of walking with God. I've seen the community it creates and the ways it strengthens faith. Our mother Lucy Sabiiti has faithfully encouraged us in it. We will forever be thankful for the ways in which they've taught us even though our father Late Eric Sabiiti Jasi is passed on and supported us in prayer, showing us what it means to have a personal relationship with Jesus.

For parents with kids of any age, remember this: Your children see you. They watch you and look up to you. They want to be like you. How amazing would it be if the next generation saw parents of prayer, and that's what they wanted to be like when they grow up? Pray for and with your children. Show them how you pray, give them a journal, pray with them at night. Your example will teach, your prayers will be heard, and your children will be encouraged.

Though we can get tired in the waiting, Father, we know that your Spirit is right alongside helping us along. If we don't know how or what to pray, it doesn't matter. He does our praying in and for us, making prayer out of our wordless sighs, our aching groans. He knows us far better than we know ourselves, knows our pregnant condition, and keeps us present before you. That's why we can be so sure that every detail in our lives of love for you is worked into something good. May we live our lives absolutely convinced that nothing—nothing living or dead, angelic or demonic, today or tomorrow, high or low, thinkable or unthinkable—absolutely nothing can get between us and your love because of the way that Jesus has embraced us. We love you Father. Amen. (Romans 8:26-28, 38).

The Following Are Publications We Have Done So Far

- Breakthrough Declarations Of A Praying Wife
- Breakthrough Declarations To Receive Money
- Yega Bible Children Bible Stories
- Increase Your Cash Flow
- The Culture Of Royal Civility
- Yega Orutooro
- Royal Civility Magazine

Sow This Book Into Someone's Life

Don't let the impact of this book end with you

www.julianbusinge.com

Contact us: royal@julianbusinge.com

Or connect on social media:

Facebook Page:

https://www.facebook.com/Royal-Civility-102394171599241

Thank you and looking forward to celebrating with you, great testimonies, Amen.

Do Not Go Yet; One Last Thing To Do

If You Liked This Book Or Found It Useful, I'd Appreciate It If You Could Leave A Quick Review On Amazon. Your Support Is Greatly Appreciated, we will Personally Read All Of The Reviews In Order To Obtain Your Feedback And Improve The Book.

Thanks For Your Help And Support!

www.ingramcontent.com/pod-product-compliance
Lightning Source LLC
Chambersburg PA
CBHW050254120526
44590CB00016B/2351